Gabriele Grünebaum

How to Marbleize Paper

Step-by-Step Instructions for 12 Traditional Patterns

Dover Publications, Inc., New York

Contents

Copyright © 1984 by Gabriele Grünebaum.
All rights reserved under Pan American and International Copyright Conventions.

Published in Canada by General Publishing Company, Ltd., 30 Lesmill Road, Don Mills, Toronto, Ontario.
Published in the United Kingdom by Constable and Company, Ltd., 10 Orange Street, London WC2H 7EG.

How to Marbleize Paper: Step-by-Step Instructions for 12 Traditional Patterns is a new work, first published by Dover Publications, Inc. in 1984.

Manufactured in the United States of America
Dover Publications, Inc., 31 East 2nd Street, Mineola, N.Y. 11501

Library of Congress Cataloging in Publication Data

Grünebaum, Gabriele.
    How to marbleize paper.

    1. Marbling (Bookbinding)   2. Paper finishing.   I. Title.
Z271.G94 1984   686.3′6   83-20566
ISBN 0-486-24651-5

Introduction

Marbleizing, also known as marbling, is a method of decorating paper through the use of "floating colors." The colors are not applied directly to the paper as is done in painting, but rather to a liquid called the marbleizing size. The patterns that form on top of the size are then removed from the size by laying a piece of paper on them.

The tradition of marbleizing goes back to the Suminagashi paper produced in eighth-century Japan. The top right corner of this writing paper was decorated in delicate hues with a small marbleized pattern. The art of marbleizing traveled to Persia and Turkey and reached Europe in the fifteenth century. There it underwent a continuous further development until it reached its high point in the late-nineteenth-century art style known as Art Nouveau or Jugendstil. Many kinds of marbleized paper were exported from the Netherlands, France and Germany at the time.

After several decades of being out of fashion, the various techniques of colored-paper production have recently been finding increasing interest among bookbinders and craftspeople. At the same time, marbleizing fabrics has also become a popular craft. Marbleized paper and fabrics can be used for decorating such traditional objects as books and boxes and for lampshades, handbags, shirts, wall hangings and other projects.

A particular charm of marbleizing is that the patterns floating on the size cannot be controlled in the most minute details, as can brushstrokes in painting. Thus, even with the greatest precision and care, it is impossible to produce two identical marbleized sheets of paper. Even minor changes in the composition and temperature of the colors and other ingredients can cause significant differences in the way the colors react to each other on the size.

This book describes all necessary steps for classic and oil-color marbleizing. Classic marbleizing, which uses water-based colors mixed with ox gall, gives vivid patterns and offers many design options. Oil-color marbleizing is easier to prepare but allows a smaller range of effects. The book is divided into two parts: the first gives general directions for the two methods, the second provides specific instructions for particular marbleized patterns.

Following an examination of the traditional marbleizing process in the first section of Part I, Sections 2–6 discuss tools and ingredients and the preparation of the size, paper and colors for classic marbleizing. Section 7 discusses oil-color marbleizing and Section 8 gives directions for marbleizing fabrics. Causes and solutions for common marbleizing mistakes are provided in the last section of Part I. Patterning recipes and examples of about a dozen marbleized papers are included in the second part of the book. Supply sources and metric conversion chart sections appear at the end of the book.

Like all artistic handicrafts, creative marbleizing requires a certain amount of time. In addition to these directions you will need patience and imagination. Experiment with different colors and patterns and follow your own tastes.

Ills. 1 & 2. "Marbreur de Papier" (The Paper Marbleizer). Taken from Diderot and d'Alembert's *Encyclopédie* (1765), these engravings show the complete marbleizing process as it was conducted two centuries ago.

PART I.

Basic Marbleizing Techniques

1. The Paper Marbleizer

The copperplate engravings on page 4 (Ills. 1 & 2) show the steps involved in marbleizing as it was done two hundred years ago. A typical workshop of the time is shown. Although only one person was usually employed in the production of marbleized paper and performed all of the operations one after the other, each one is done in the illustrations by a different worker (Figs. 1–11) in order to show all steps of the marbleizing process.

On the right in Ill. 1, Fig. 1 is preparing the marbleizing size. On the other side of the room, the man at the second window (Fig. 3) is dripping colors onto the size with a small brush. In front of him, Fig. 4 is drawing a comb through the color drops on the size to create the pattern for snail marbleized paper. The floating pattern is transferred (Fig. 5) to the paper by laying a sheet on the size. In the background (Fig. 8) the wet sheets are being hung up on lines to dry. At the left (Fig. 2), pigments are being ground and pulverized for the production of marbleizing colors—a chore done nowadays by art-supply manufacturers.

On the left side of Ill. 2 we see two bookbinders. The man in the rear (Fig. 11, No. 1) is forming the patterns on the size with a stick. The man in front (Fig. 11, No. 2) is dipping the books in a tray to transfer the patterns to the book edges. Nowadays this time-consuming work is rarely performed by bookbinderies.

To preserve fine paper after the colors have been applied, it is again drawn through a thin glue solution and dried. This is being done in the rear of the workshop by the man at center (Fig. 10, No. 2). On the right side of the room paper is being pressed smooth. Fig. 9 is rubbing paper with a waxed wool cloth. Behind him a worker (Fig. 10, No. 1) is smoothing it with an agate stone. Only particularly rough paper was treated in this way. The paper we use nowadays does not require smoothing.

2. Workplace, Tools and Materials

Marbleized paper is produced basically the same way today as it was two hundred years ago. The most important tools and ingredients are shown in the old copperplate engravings on pages 6 and 7 (Ills. 3 & 4). They include trays for holding the size, brushes for color dropping, combs for pattern forming and a workbench with many tools for smoothing, decorating and drying paper. It is advisable to set up your workplace near a water faucet since water is frequently needed for rinsing the marbleized paper and cleaning tools.

The following materials are used in classic marbleizing:

Large pot
Marbleizing tray
Coarse sieve
Fine cloth (nylon stocking, towel, etc.)
Large container
Wooden sticks
Distilled water
Drop brushes and pipettes
Marbleizing combs
Small pot
Alum
Paper
Newspaper
Paint containers
Marbling colors
Ox gall
Moss preservative (optional)
Carrageen moss (Irish moss)
Various chemicals (as stated for certain patterns)

The Supply Sources section on page 30 lists places where carrageen moss, ox gall, marbling colors and other materials can be obtained.

The colors, paper and size ingredients used in classic marbleizing are discussed in the following sections. Once you have the items listed above, you can begin to prepare the ingredients and materials.

A large pot is needed for boiling the carrageen moss for the size. How large a pot you will need depends on the capacity of your marbleizing tray. For the directions given for size preparation in Section 3, a pot with a 3-gallon capacity will do. After boiling, the moss mixture is strained through a coarse sieve and then through a fine cloth to remove all solid residue from the size. The straining can be done into any large container. After it has set, the size is poured into the marbleizing tray.

The classic marbleizing tray is a 3″-deep sheet-zinc basin, but simple plastic trays, such as those used in photo laboratories, are well suited for marbleizing. Trays are available in many different widths and lengths—20 × 26″ is an average size—but they should be somewhat larger than the paper you are marbleizing. The more expensive metal or wood trays have a separate overflow compartment at one end for collecting the color residue and other

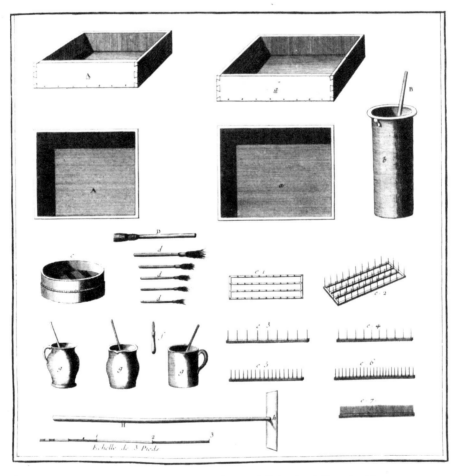

Ill. 3. Traditional marbleizing tools shown in Diderot and d'Alembert's *Encyclopédie*.

waste products. This feature is not essential; residue can be scraped into any long container.

You should have on hand enough wooden sticks to stir the colors in their separate containers. The colors are mixed with a dispersing agent, ox gall, which keeps them from sinking into the size. If the colors need to be diluted, a little distilled water can be added.

In addition to simple wooden sticks, marbleizing combs are necessary for forming some color patterns such as those on the comb marbleized paper. A few types of marbleizing combs can be bought from suppliers, but handy, inexpensive ones can be made at home. Instructions for making different types of combs are given on pages 18, 20 and 22. Alum, copper vitriol, blood albumen and other chemicals used as separating agents will be required for some patterns.

To apply the colors and chemicals to the size, drop brushes, pipettes or sticks are required, at least one for each mixture. Drop brushes, which are good for shaking a large amount of color onto the size, are usually made out of camel's hair or straw. An inexpensive homemade alternative to the drop brush is one made out of broom or drinking straws. It can be made by binding a handful of straws together with a string, rubber band or tape. The straws should be at least 8″ long and bound in the middle to leave a 4″ handle.

A small pot is used in preparing the alum solution with which the paper is treated before marbleizing so that colors will adhere to the surface of the paper. The solution is applied with a soft sponge to the side of the paper being marbleized. If both sides are being decorated, the paper can be drawn through a shallow tray filled with the solution.

When the size has stood untouched for a while and before each application of color on its surface, the size is cleaned by skimming the surface film over the end of the trough. Narrow strips of newspaper or cardboard can be used for skimming; make many strips because they rarely can be used more than once.

Tools and containers should be cleaned after using. Dirt, oil and residue from the various mixtures can adversely affect the colors and size and ruin your patterns. Some suppliers offer surgical gloves and protective cream for people whose skin is sensitive to the colors and chemicals used in marbleizing.

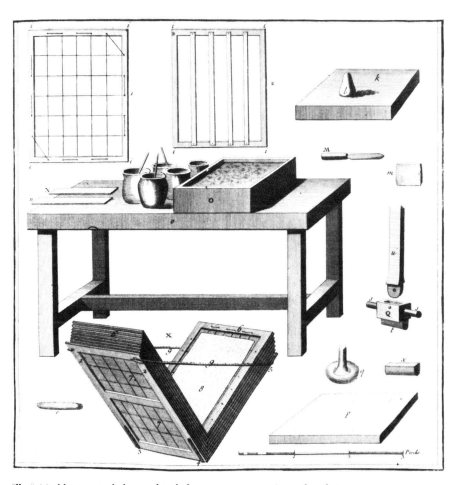

Ill. 4. Marbleizing workplace and tools for preparing paper *(Encyclopédie)*.

3. The Marbleizing Size

The first step in classic marbleizing is the preparation of the size, the thickened solution of vegetable matter to which the colors are applied. A mistake frequently made by beginning marbleizers is the failure to appreciate the importance of the preparation and treatment of the size. Colors will not react well on unproperly prepared size. Age, temperature and composition all affect the size's consistency.

The classic marbleizing size is commonly made with a dried seaweed, carrageen moss, also known as Irish moss. Carrageen-moss size should be made at least a day in advance of marbleizing.

Carrageen-Moss Size Recipe

8 qts. water (very hard water should be mixed with ½ oz. of borax)
5 oz. carrageen moss
8 Tbs. size preservative (35% formaldehyde solution)
2 qts. cold water

Pour the 8 qts. of water into a large pot and stir in the moss. Add the size preservative if you are planning to keep the size for longer than four days. Cook the mixture for about 10 minutes, stirring it when it boils. Add the cold water to the hot brew. After the liquid has cooled, pour it through a sieve and strain it through a fine cloth to remove the solid residue. The strained size can be used after it has lain covered in a cool place for 24 hours and has become slightly gelatinous. The size is poured into the marbleizing tray, filling it to at least a 1″ depth. Surplus size should be covered and set aside. The size and the tray should both be at room temperature.

Carrageenam, a prepared extract of the seaweed, can also be used for making the size. It does not need to be boiled or strained. You simply mix it in a blender—4 Tbs. of carrageenam will be enough for about 10 qts. of size. Carrageenam costs about three times as much as carrageen moss, but you may find the convenience well worth the price. It is available from many distributors of marbleizing supplies.

4. Colors and Ox Gall

Classic marbling (marbleizing) colors are made from very finely ground pigments mixed with distilled water. Nowadays many different marbling colors are available, usually in liquid forms and are recommended because you can be sure that the pigments have been ground fine enough to prevent them from sinking into the size. For your first marbleized projects it is best to prepare only one or two colors. Each of the prepared colors must be tested again and again on the size, and adjusted if necessary, until it is of the right composition to float and spread out properly.

To keep the colors floating on the size and prevent them from mixing with each other, they are combined with prepared ox gall. A few tablespoons of color mixed with several drops of ox gall will be enough. The colors can be diluted with distilled water if they are too thick to work with easily. The colors, ox gall and distilled water should all be at room temperature.

Before testing the colors, make sure that the size is satisfactory. Surface film should be skimmed off with a newspaper strip because film and any other residue left in the size will prevent the colors from spreading properly.

The size should be at room temperature—sizes that are too cool will cause the colors to sink; sizes that are too warm will cause the colors to spread far apart. If necessary, a little cold or warm water can be added to the size and gently but thoroughly stirred in. If, despite all adjustments with the colors, they will not spread out or float, it is possible that the size is too thick and needs to be thinned with some room-temperature water. Thick sizes trap colors in heavy concentrations that sink. Thin sizes, on the other hand, do not hold the colors in the desired pattern satisfactorily.

When all is ready, put a large drop of color with the mixing stick on the surface of the size. The color drop should spread out to form a circle of about 3″. If too little ox gall has been added to the color, the drop will not spread enough and will sink. The correct composition can be produced by adding the ox gall to the color mixture drop by drop and then retesting it on the size. If the color drops expand too much, the proportion of ox gall is too high and more marbling color from the bottle should be added to the mixture.

5. Paper

Paper used in marbleizing is exposed to hard tests. In classic marbleizing, the sheet is moistened with an alum solution, laid on the colors in the size bath and pulled out of the tray by two corners. To prevent tearing, you should always use firm paper such as papier Ingres or vat paper, but packing and typing paper are also suitable. The paper can be white or colored. Trimming the paper will be necessary if it is too wide to fit in the tray with inches to spare on all sides.

To make the colors stick to the sheet, the paper must be given an even coating of an alum solution before it is marbleized. To make the solution, 3.5 oz. of alum crystals are poured into a quart of boiling water and dissolved. Be careful to measure correctly; an overly concentrated alum solution can cause colors to flake off the paper. When the solution is cool, the side of the sheet to which the color is to be applied is dampened evenly with a sponge. If you wish to make the paper a little firmer or marbleize it on both sides, the solution can be poured into a tray and the sheets dipped in it.

After the paper has been treated with the solution, it is laid out to dry. Place a weighted sheet of cardboard on top of the paper while it dries to keep it flat and prevent wrinkling.

The paper should not be completely dry when the patterns are applied to it; it can be worked with more easily if still a little damp.

Paper is usually prepared in batches. After marbleizing the first sheet in the batch, you may discover that your alum solution was too strong and the colors are flaking off the sheet. You can still use the rest of the papers in the batch if you first apply a thin solution of wallpaper paste to the alumed sides of the sheets before marbleizing.

6. Classic Marbleizing

Classic marbleized paper is produced basically the same way as is described in Section 1. After the size has been skimmed, the paper prepared, colors tested and all necessary tools are ready, you can begin creating marbleized patterns. Drops of color are applied to the surface of the size where they spread out but do not mix with each other. The method used for patterning the colors on the size will vary according to which type of marbleized paper you are making. Drop brushes, sticks or pipettes are used for dropping the colors. Combs,

Ill. 5. Colors are sprinkled onto the size from a drop brush.

Ill. 6. A stick is drawn through the colors to form parallel lines.

Ill. 7. A fine-tooth comb is drawn from right to left through the colors to make a comb pattern.

Ill. 8. A peacock board is drawn through the comb pattern in a snaking, zigzag motion to make a peacock pattern.

Ill. 9. Held by diagonally opposite corners, a sheet of paper is laid on the colors.

Ill. 10. After lying on the colors for a moment, the marbleized sheet is lifted off the size. It is then rinsed and dried.

sticks and chemicals are used for making patterns.

Illustrations 5–10 show the basic steps for making one type of pattern—in this case, that for peacock marbleized paper. In Ill. 5, the colors are being sprinkled on the size from a drop brush. The brush is dipped into a paint container and held above the size. Colors are then shaken onto the size or the brush is tapped so that many drops fall at once. Separate brushes are required for each color used. The color that is sprinkled on first usually spreads out the most.

In Ill. 6, the end of a paintbrush is being used as a stick to draw lines across the surface of the size. The colors form a series of arrowheads pointing in the direction that the stick is being drawn. The drawing should be done lightly so as not to disturb the size, and the points of sticks or comb teeth should not be allowed to dip below the surface of the size. Drawn smoothly across the tray from right to left, the points of a fine-tooth comb are shown leaving a typical comb pattern in the colors in Ill. 7. Combs and comb patterns are described on page 18. Ill. 8 shows a peacock board being drawn from right to left in a back-and-forth snaking motion to make a peacock pattern similar to the one shown on the front cover. Patterns should be formed fairly quickly. As soon as you have a satisfactory pattern, transfer it to the paper before it changes or starts to sink.

When the pattern is ready, the alumed paper is lifted by diagonally opposite corners as shown in Ill. 9. Without folding or creasing the paper, lay it slowly and carefully on top of the colors in a smooth, even movement. If the paper is laid too abruptly, ripples can form on the size and cause the colors to come together in wave-like patterns that cover the paper unevenly. This effect is desirable when making wave marbled paper, but you can also unintentionally destroy other patterns. You should be particularly careful to lay the paper smoothly so that no small air bubbles form between the size and the paper. Air bubbles interfere with the color transfer and cause white spots to appear on the paper.

Patterns are transferred to the paper at first contact. As soon as the entire surface has been marbleized, lift up the paper by one end, as shown in Ill. 10, and remove it from the size. Rinse the sheet with running water to cleanse it of any remaining size residue, or, if no faucet is handy, wipe the paper with a damp sponge. After the sheet has been cleaned, it is laid out flat or hung up to dry. The finished paper can then be used for any number of decorative projects or be hung up to admire. Waxes and varnishes are available that will give the paper a hard finish.

Before the marbleizing size can be used for new patterns, it must be cleansed of all color remnants, some of which float on the surface as small particles. Take a strip of newspaper or cardboard and push the remaining floating colors to one end of the tray. There they can be scooped into an overflow box or over the edge of the tray. A film will appear on size that has not been used for a while. Be sure to skim it off before applying more colors to the size.

7. Oil-Color Marbleizing

The methods for producing classic marbleized paper and oil-color marbleized paper are very similar, but the ingredients used are considerably different. Less preparation is necessary for oil-color marbleizing, but your control over the patterns is limited. The technique for applying and patterning oil colors is described on page 28.

For oil-color marbleizing, the paper does not have to be treated with alum and it does not have to be washed with water after the transfer of the floating patterns.

A size of pure tap water is sufficient for oil-color marbleizing. If you like delicate patterns or wish to control the colors better, a little paste can be added to the water to make it more viscous. Colors will move more slowly on the thickened size. To make the paste-water size, a handful of wallpaper paste, stirred until it is creamy, is dissolved in 5 qts. of water and stirred again to keep clumps from forming. (The wallpaper paste is usually made from wheat starch, but other thickeners can also be used.) The paste-water mixture should be used immediately after it is prepared.

Oil colors in tubes and lacquer and lino-cut colors are suitable. The colors are diluted with turpentine or turpentine substitute until watery. Turpentine acts as a dispersing agent. As with the colors in classic marbleizing, oil colors need to be tested by applying drops to the size. The drops should expand a little and form an extremely thin coating on the size. If the color sinks, it needs more turpentine; if it spreads way out, it needs more oil color. The floating colors form a barely discernible film on the size, but they show up clearly when transferred to paper.

8. Marbleizing Fabrics

Patterns can be transferred onto some fabrics using the same basic technique as that for oil marbleizing. 100% silk, cotton or taffeta are all suitable for marbleizing. These materials should be prewashed and dried before they are used. They do not have to be treated with alum. Oil colors or the textile colors used for batik and fabric printing can be used for marbleizing. Oil colors can be diluted with turpentine; textile colors should be diluted with the substance recommended on the package.

The size and colors are prepared as described in the directions for oil-color marbleizing. As soon as the pattern has been formed on the colors, the fabric is laid on top of the size and then lifted off and laid out flat on newspapers to dry. The decorated fabric is good for pillows, handbags, scarves, shirts and many other uses.

9. Mistakes: Causes and Solutions

PROBLEM	CAUSES	SOLUTIONS
White spots—places that have not received any color—on the paper.	Air bubbles formed between the paper and the size.	Paper must be laid on the size more carefully; do not crease or bend the sheet.
The color does not spread on the size or sinks to the bottom of the tray.	(1) The color is too thick; or (2) too little dispersing agent (ox gall or turpentine) was used; or (3) a film has formed on the size (if it has been standing for a while); or (4) paint particles are still floating on the size.	(1) Dilute the color with distilled water; (2) add more dispersing agent; (3) skim off the film; (4) remove the paint particles from the size.
The color spreads too much on the size.	The color is too thin or it contains too much dispersing agent.	Add more color from the tube or bottle to the color mixture.
The colors come off when the paper is washed.	(1) The paper was not treated with alum; or (2) the paper was too damp when laid on the size.	(1) Treat the paper with alum solution; (2) let it dry longer after applying the solution.
After the paper is laid on the size and set aside to dry, the colors flake off in some places.	(1) The alum solution was too concentrated; or (2) the paper was dried on a radiator.	In the future (1) use the correct alum solution and (2) allow the paper to dry slowly.

PART II.

Recipes

The recipes for marbleized papers given in the second half of this book are intended as basic guides only. No two marbleized patterns are ever exactly alike, and your pattern may look quite different from the examples shown here. Experiment with colors and use the patterning tools and ingredients listed at the beginning of each recipe to create different effects. The first ten recipes can be used for classic marbleizing, the last two for oil-color marbleizing.

Fantasy Marbleized Paper

Wooden sticks, drop brush

Fantasy marbleized paper is made by letting the colors form patterns on the size with little or no manipulation. The basic form of the floating colors is created through the random or symmetrical application of one or more colors with brushes, sticks or pipettes.

The pattern that appears depends on how many colors are used, how much ox gall has been added to them, and where and in what amount they are dropped on the size. The patterns made by dropping the colors on the size are often quite charming and you may wish to transfer them at once without any manipulation. The colors can, however, be moved around a little with a wooden stick. Lines can be made, as shown in Ill. 6, by dipping the point in the surface of the size and pulling the colors in the desired direction. The thicker the size, the more slowly the colors move on it and the better they can be manipulated.

The paper shown below was made by moving a stick in all directions until an irregular pattern reminiscent of marble resulted.

Stone Marbleized Paper

Drop brushes, ox gall, oil (olive, linseed or almond)

The pattern of stone marbleized paper is composed of small spots, giving it the appearance of a pebbled surface. Usually only one or two colors are used.

To make this paper, the colors are sprinkled on the size from a drop brush so that many small drops fall at the same time. The more numerous the small drops of color, the less room they have to spread. The drops form color spots separated by small white veins.

The width of the veins can be controlled to some degree by adding a small amount of oil to colors before applying them to the size. The more oil you add to the colors, the narrower the veins become. The oil should, however, be used sparingly and added to the color one drop at a time.

If you want the veins to be very clear, sprinkle a solution of one part ox gall to ten parts distilled water over the colors on the size.

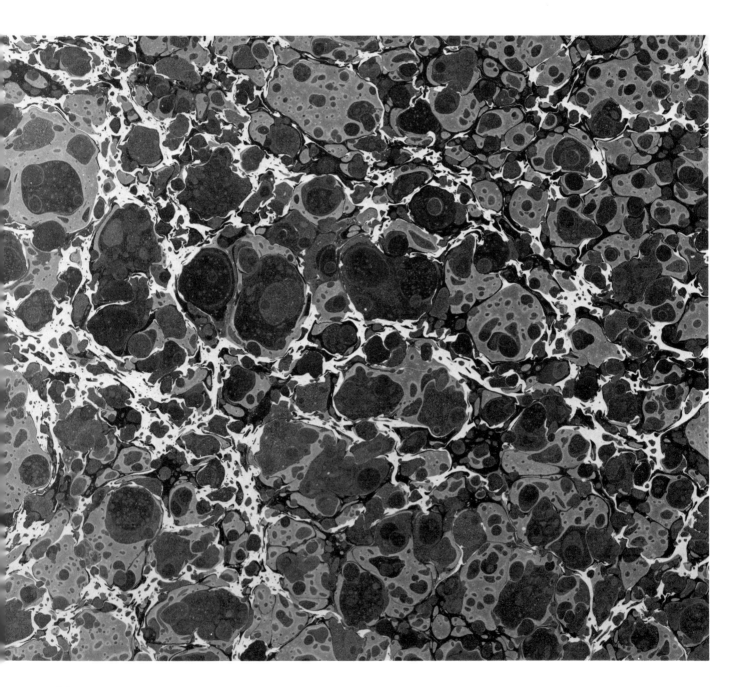

Swedish Marbleized Paper

Turpentine oil (rectified turpentine) in addition to materials listed for stone marbleized paper

Basically a stone marbleized pattern with small granular drops on it, Swedish marbleized paper is made by dripping turpentine oil on the colors. First a stone marbleized pattern is made on the size following the directions on page 14. Undiluted turpentine oil is then dripped on the size from a brush. Wherever the oil drops fall, the typical black-and-white grainy spots develop.

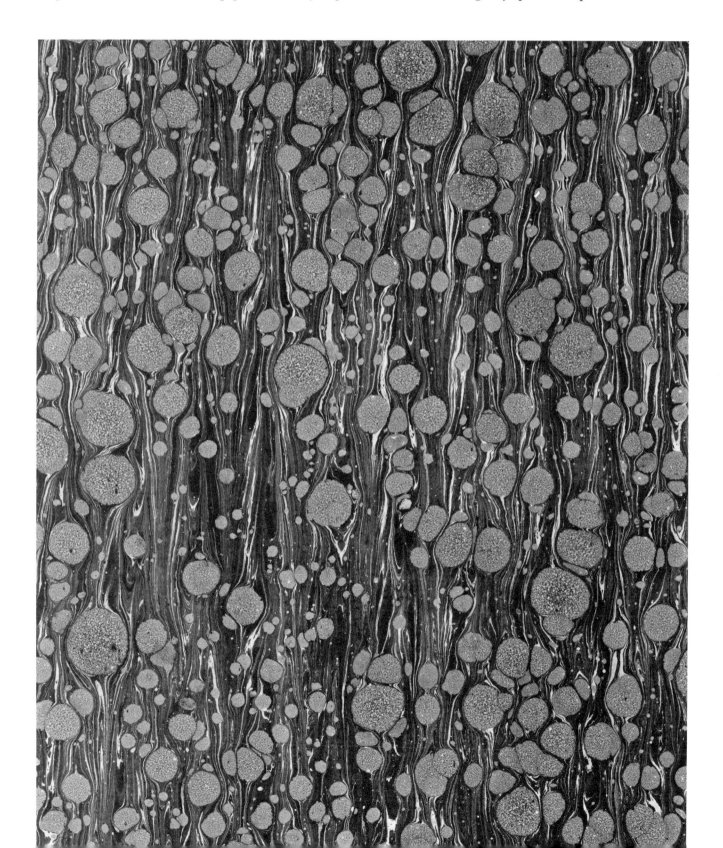

Wave Marbleized Paper

Two wooden sticks that are at least as long as the width of the marbleizing tray and whatever materials are needed for making the ground pattern

Wave effects can be added to any other pattern. They are produced either by moving the tray on its rollers to slightly agitate the size or by moving the paper as you are laying it on the size.

If you are using the roller method, you must first place the tray on two sticks that will allow it to be rocked back and forth. When the size is still, colors are applied to it until the surface is covered. The pattern you have chosen is then made on the size. When the pattern is satisfactory, small waves can be produced in the colors on the size by gently rolling the tray back and forth on its sticks. The colors will follow the movements of the size, coming

together in darker areas on the tops of waves, spreading out between waves to form light areas. When the size is no longer moving, the pattern can be transferred to a sheet of paper where the wave effect in the colors will be more evident.

The irregular waves on the paper below were made by rolling the tray on sticks. The straight, parallel lines on the veined paper at right were made by jerking the paper on the size.

A wave effect can also be achieved by moving a sheet of paper abruptly when transferring a pattern to it. Sometimes this happens unintentionally when the laying of the paper on the size has not been practiced. If the paper is placed on the size with a uniform but jerky movement, the color will form parallel stripes.

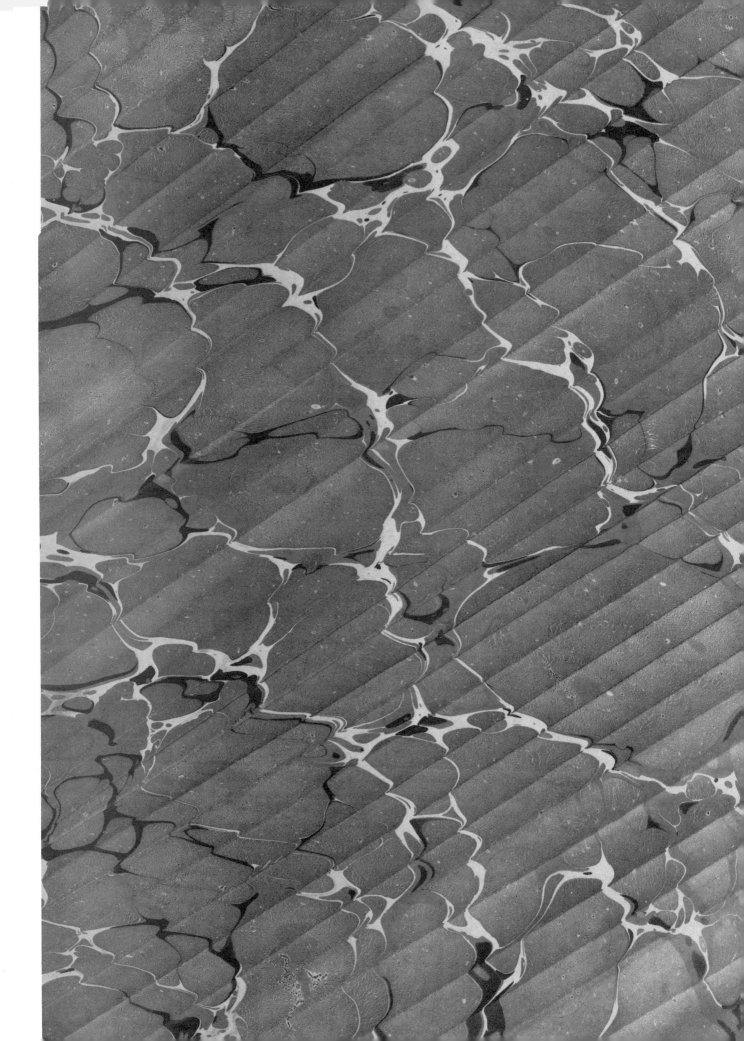

Comb Marbleized Paper

Wooden sticks, marbleizing combs

Comb marbleized paper is one of the traditional old marbleized patterns and was common in Europe as early as the seventeenth century. To make it you will need marbleizing combs. Some combs, usually with fixed teeth, can be bought from marbleizing suppliers, but most of the ones used for the patterns in this book will need to be handmade.

The basic marbleizing comb is made from a board or strip of wood that is at least ¼″ thick, 2″ wide and 2″ longer than the width of the tray. Small holes are drilled at ³⁄₁₆″ or ¼″ intervals in the edge of the board for the comb's teeth. The teeth can be nails, hair-curler pins or other pieces of metal with heads, and should be 3″ or more in length. The teeth should fit firmly in the holes and their points should protrude at least 1″ out of the wood. A couple of coats of lacquer will protect the comb against dampness and warping. A saw, drill and tape measure will be necessary to make this comb; a drill stand will make it much easier to drill the small 2″-long holes with a power tool more accurately.

Depending on the pattern you desire, pins can be put in every hole, put in every other hole or placed in pairs. Ill. 11 shows three possible arrangements. An endless number of combed patterns can be made by changing the positions of the teeth. Fine combed lines can be made by spacing the teeth at intervals of ¼″ or less; wide-toothed combs with ½–3″ gaps will make broader patterns.

Simpler, fixed-tooth combs can be made with two strips of ⅛″-thick cardboard or plywood, 2″-long pins or needles, glue and an X-ACTO or utility knife. The strips should be 2″ wide and of any convenient length, but cardboard should not be used for very long combs. Draw a line down the middle of one of the strips dividing the 2″ width in

half. If you are using pins, cut a groove along the line for the pinheads. Next, mark off lines for inserting the pins (see Ill. 12) at the desired even or irregular intervals. Cut slots that will allow the pins to be embedded in the strip without being loose. Glue the pins in the slots so that they protrude 1″ from the bottom of the strip, then glue the second strip over the first, sealing the pins in between. The comb should be left to dry with a heavy object on top of it and then given a coat of varnish.

There are many ways to make patterns for comb marbleized paper—Ills. 5–7 show one possibility. Usually, exact instructions are given for making the pattern; here, however, the approach given is meant only as a suggestion.

First, a color is applied symmetrically, drop by drop, to the size. Drops of a second color are then placed in the middle of the first color's spreading circles. In the middle of the second color's circles, a third color (or the first color again) is placed. This process is repeated until the concentric, equally large color rings have covered the size. The marbleizing comb is then placed on one side of the tray so that its ends rest on the tray's top and bottom edges. The comb's teeth are dipped at an angle into the surface of the size and the comb is then drawn slowly across the tray, as shown in Ill. 7. The teeth pull at the colors and form the typical comb marbleized pattern. Because the comb rests partially on the edge of the tray, it can be drawn easily and in a straight line.

For a variation of the comb marbleized pattern, you can repeat the process just described in reverse direction. After you have drawn the comb through the colors to one side of the tray, move it slightly toward the top or bottom edge, about half the distance between two teeth, and draw it back across the tray to the starting point. This results in the reverse comb pattern.

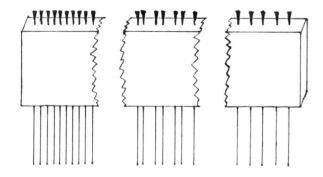

Ill. 11. Sections from combs showing three different arrangements of the teeth.

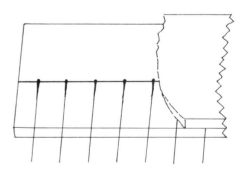

Ill. 12. Cross section of a cardboard-and-pin comb.

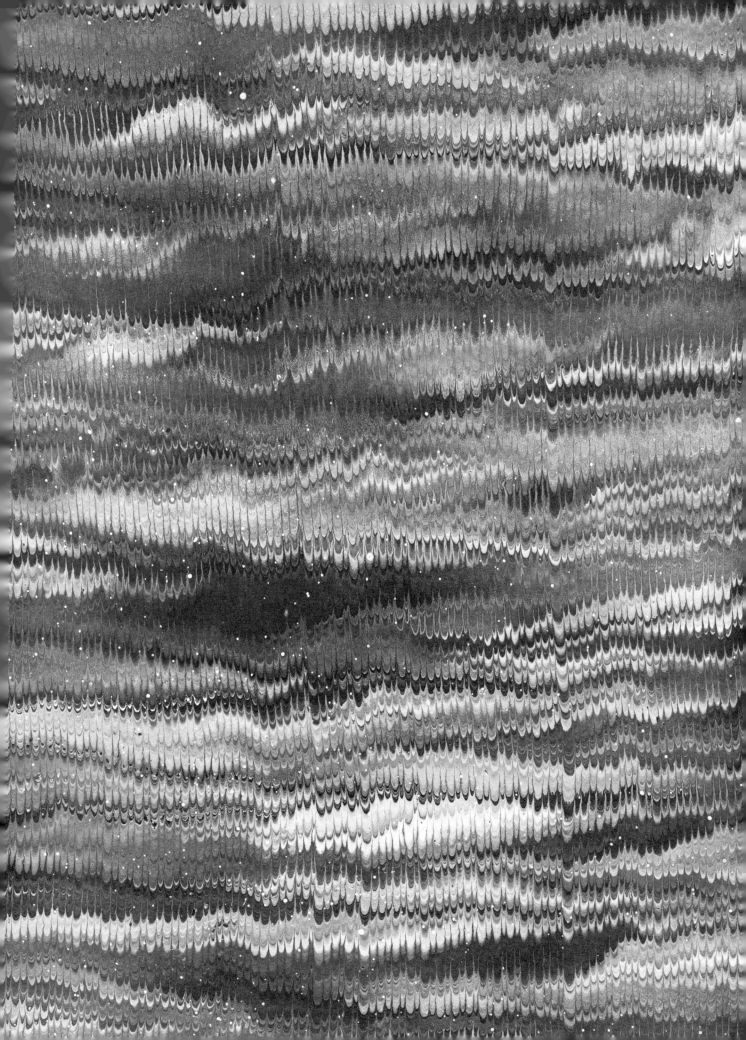

Snail Pattern Marbleized Paper

Wooden sticks and a small nail-studded board

Snail marbleized paper can be recognized by the many spirals in its pattern, which is also known as French Curl. The spirals can either be formed one at a time with a stick or in groups with a board.

First, the size is either completely covered with colors randomly distributed in a fantasy-paper type pattern (see page 13), or a comb pattern is used as a starting point for the snail pattern (see page 18). The spirals can then be formed individually by using the wooden sticks to stir the colors into smaller and smaller circles. This must be repeated for each spiral until the pattern is complete and ready to be transferred.

With the nail board the snail pattern can be created evenly and in a single movement for the whole paper. The board is made by pushing several rows of nails or similar pieces of metal through a small wooden board or thick cardboard. The board's width and length should both be 4″ smaller than that of the marbleizing tray. The nails or pins must be steady and either fit exactly or be glued in place. The distance between the nails can be between 1″ and 3″ depending on how large you want the spirals to be. The board should be given several coats of lacquer before using to protect it from moisture.

To make the snail pattern, hold the board over the size with its edges equidistant from the sides of the tray. The teeth are then lowered into the colors and the board is drawn in a spiraling movement.

If you find a large nail board to be too heavy and hard to handle, use a strip of wood with protruding nails instead and make several rows of spirals.

Fig. 4 in Ill. 1 is making a snail pattern with a nail board.

Snail pattern marbleized paper is shown in color on the front cover.

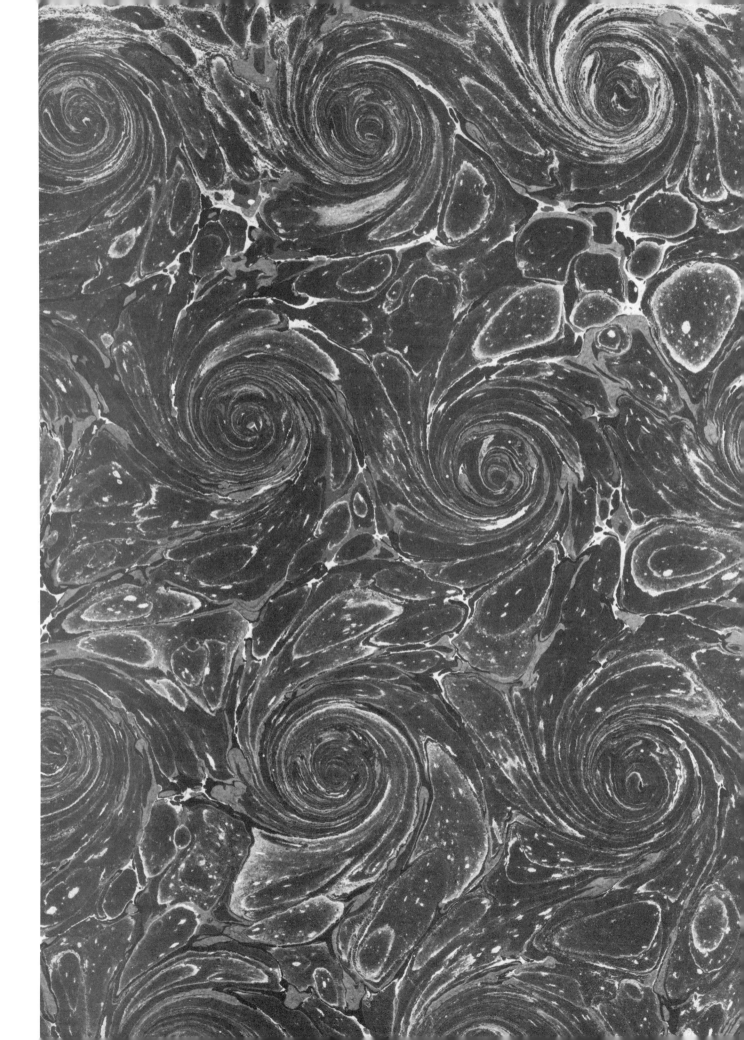

Bouquet Marbleized Paper
and
Peacock Marbleized Paper

Fine-tooth and wide-toothed marbleizing combs, peacock board or peacock comb

The patterns of bouquet and peacock marbleized paper are a further development of comb marbleized paper. The bouquet and peacock patterns are very similar, but peacock is finer and requires a special tool.

To make the bouquet pattern, two different marbleizing combs—one wide-toothed, one fine-tooth—are needed. First, a normal comb pattern is made with a wide-toothed comb (see p. 18), then the fine-tooth comb is drawn in the same direction in a snaking, zigzag motion to make the bouquet pattern. On page 23 is an example of bouquet marbleized paper. It is shown in color on the top of the back inside cover.

The peacock pattern is made with a marbleizing comb and a peacock comb or board. The patterns made with the peacock comb and a peacock board are almost identical, but making and using the peacock comb is considerably more difficult.

The peacock board is composed of two similar wide-toothed marbleizing combs glued together. The board should be about 2″ shorter than the width of the tray and its two rows of teeth should be aligned as shown in Ill. 13, with the rows shifted half the distance between two teeth. The teeth can be 1″ to 3″ apart; the rows will be anywhere from ¼″ to 2″ apart depending on the thickness of the

combs used to make the board. The peacock board can also be made by drilling two or more rows of holes in a board and inserting nails. The holes should be carefully measured and aligned as in Ill. 13 and the nails should be firmly embedded in the wood.

The peacock comb also consists of two marbleizing combs that are about 2″ shorter than the tray's width. The combs are connected in such a way that they can be slid parallel to each other back and forth in opposite directions. One of the many possible constructions is shown in Ill. 14. A groove is made in the side of one comb and a strip of wood that will fit and slide easily in the groove is attached to the other comb. Two metal strips are then fastened with screws to one comb and then bent over the top and down the side of the other comb to form a U-shape that holds the combs together. The two small wood strips on the top of one comb determine how far the combs can move in opposite directions.

To make a peacock pattern, the colors on the size are given a simple comb pattern such as that shown in Ill. 7. If the peacock board is used, it is drawn through the colors with a zigzag movement in the same direction that the comb was pulled. If the peacock comb is used, the two halves of the comb are slid back and forth as they are moved slowly over the size.

Peacock marbleized paper is shown in color on the back cover.

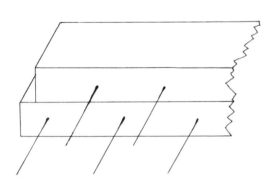

Ill. 13. Section of a peacock board showing arrangement of teeth.

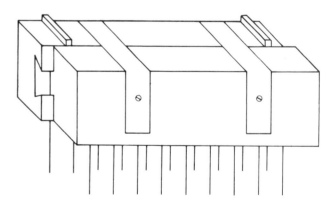

Ill. 14. Peacock comb.

Floral Pattern Marbleized Paper

Wooden sticks, needles; alum, albumen (egg white) and tartaric acid are optional

This flowered paper and other kinds of marbleized papers that have objects such as fish and birds in their patterns are among the most popular papers from the Art Nouveau period. The colors are formed into the desired shapes on the size with wooden sticks or small needles. The thicker the size, the more delicately and precisely can the colors be formed into flowers.

One or more colors are first applied to the size drop by drop, then the needles or sticks are used to draw the colors apart or together. The sticks must be moved slowly and carefully to prevent the size from moving too much and mixing the colors in an undesired way.

Another way to create flowers and blossom patterns is to mix individual colors with chemicals. The reaction of these colors on the size usually produces very imaginative forms. Adding alum to the color will make it break up and form blossom patterns on the size. Albumen will make colors form starry, aster-like blossoms. A drop of tartaric acid will cause the colors to form a radiating pattern.

Minor deviations from the reactions described here can result if the temperature of all the ingredients is not the same. The rule for using chemicals is: the thinner the size, the farther the blossoms will drift apart.

Floral pattern marbleized paper is shown in color on the bottom of the back inside cover.

Veined Marbleized Paper

Drop brush and the chemicals and ingredients mentioned for the four separating agents listed below

Veined marbleized paper usually has two sharply contrasting colors. Lines that look like fine veins cover the paper. These lines are formed when a color mixed with a separating agent is sprinkled on a color already on the size.

There are different ways of preparing the separating agents.

1. Mix equal amounts of ox gall and distilled water together.

2. Dissolve 3 oz. of alum crystals in a quart of boiling water; let it cool before using.

3. Dissolve 1½ oz. of shellac in a quart of boiling water, then add 1½ oz. of liquid ammonia; let it cool before using.

4. Use soap spirit.

Equal amounts of a separating agent and a color should be mixed together. The color should contrast sharply with the color already on the size.

The basic color is applied to the size first, then the separating agent/color mixture is shaken onto the floating colors from a drop brush in many small drops. A pattern of veins will form on the colors. The smaller the drops, the finer the network of veins will be.

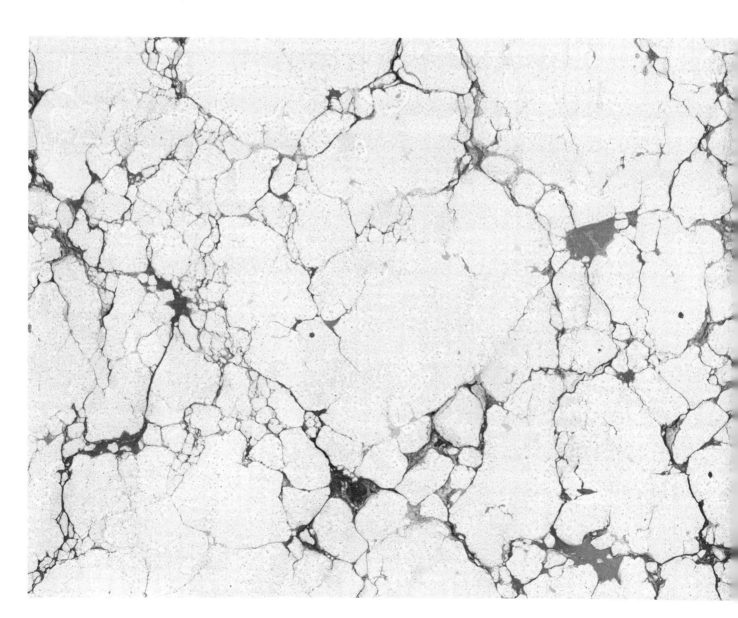

Tiger Marbleized Paper

Wooden sticks and the ingredients for the solutions mentioned below

Also called tiger eyes or sun-ray marbleized paper, tiger marbleized paper, with its fine pattern, is a result of the reaction of the floating colors and chemicals that are added to them drop by drop. The reactions produce small patterns similar to suns or tiger eyes.

The patterns develop differently depending on the composition of the colors you use. The exact reaction of the chemicals cannot be precisely predicted.

The most beautiful patterns can be created with the following solutions:

1. Dissolve some blood albumen in water and mix the result with several drops of copper vitriol.

2. Dissolve equal amounts of potash, alum and soda in warm water and permit the solution to cool before using.

The pattern created by the first solution is slightly reddish. To make the type of pattern shown below, apply the different colors to the size with a brush or pipette and use sticks to form the resulting circles into lines parallel to the sides of the tray, as in Ill. 6. This produces the basic striped structure which is given its tiger eyes by the drop-by-drop application with a drop brush of one of the solutions described above. The paper on the facing page was given a veined pattern (see page 25) before the tiger-eye solution was applied.

The striped tiger marbleized paper is shown in color on the bottom of the front inside cover.

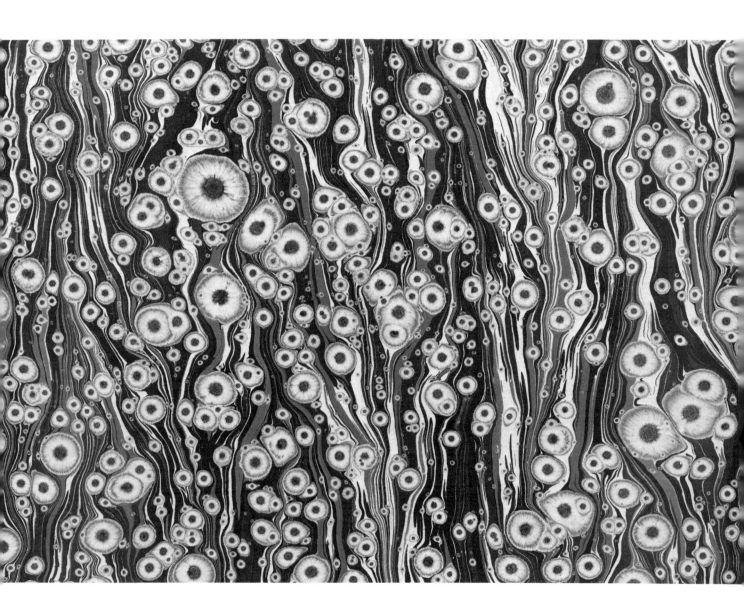

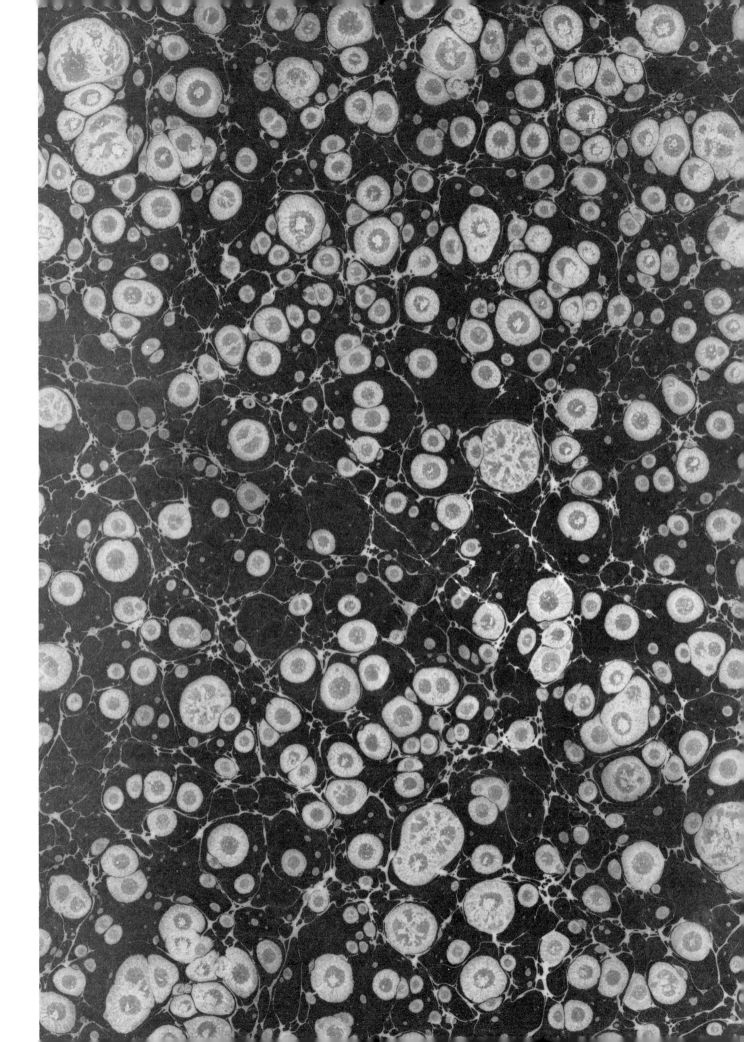

Oil-Color Marbleized Paper

Wooden sticks and other materials mentioned on page 11

The technique for making oil-color marbleized paper is basically the same as that used for water-based colors. The diluted oil colors are applied drop by drop to the water size or sprinkled on with a drop brush. When the colors separate on the surface of the water they usually break up into many small droplets recognizable as dark spots. For this reason and because the oil colors move quickly on the surface of the water or paste–water size, they are difficult to form into patterns. With the help of wooden sticks, the colors can be moved a little on the size. You have to quickly transfer any color patterns you make to the paper, otherwise the colors will separate almost immediately and form new patterns.

Oil colors need a long time to dry on paper; therefore, to avoid smearing the colors, be careful not to touch the patterns too soon.

Oil-Color Batik Marbleized Paper

Wax crayon or candle, clothes iron and lots of newspaper

Marbleizing with oil colors can be combined with the batik technique to create beautiful, unexpected patterns. In this process, certain parts of the paper are prepared in such a way that they do not absorb colors.

With a wax crayon or candle, drawings are made on the sheet of paper before it is used for marbleizing. After a pattern is made on the size, the paper is laid on the colors in the usual manner. The unwaxed parts of the sheet will absorb color while the waxed areas remain blank.

After the paper has dried, the wax is ironed out. The sheet is placed between several layers of newspaper and ironed until the wax melts and is absorbed by the newspaper.

The paper on the facing page is an example of simple oil-color marbleized paper. No oil-color batik marbleized paper is illustrated in this book.

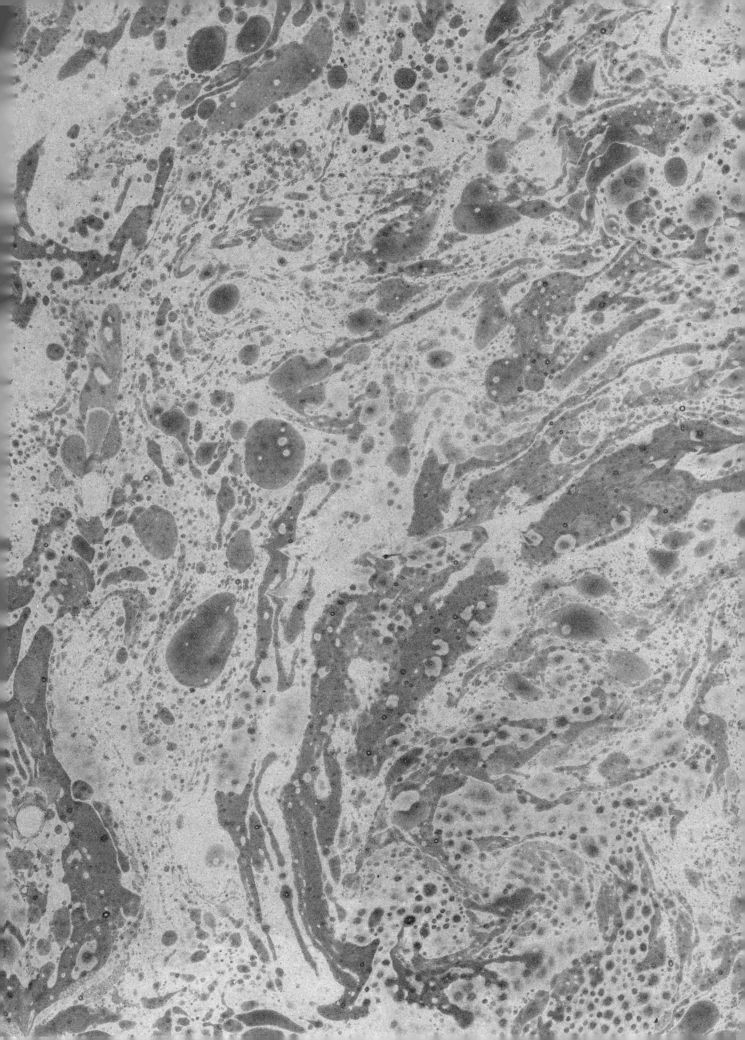

Supply Sources

Check the yellow pages for local craft-supply outlets that stock marbleizing equipment. Most art-supply and craft stores sell oil colors, ox gall, turpentine products, brushes, pipettes, paper and many of the chemicals mentioned in this book. Some art-supply stores may sell carrageen moss. Sponges, wooden sticks, pots, sieves, towels, trays and distilled water can be found in supermarkets, pharmacies or household-goods stores. It is best to obtain marbling colors, combs and ox gall from businesses that specialize in marbleizing supplies, such as those listed below. Special chemicals can be obtained from chemists and pharmacies.

If you cannot obtain special marbleizing materials from local businesses, you may wish to write to the following mail-order firms for their catalogs and supply lists.

In North America:

Basic Crafts Co., 1201 Broadway, New York, New York 10001

Colophon Hand Bookbindery, 1902 North 44th Street, Seattle, Washington 98103

TALAS, 213 West 35th Street, New York, New York 10001

In England:

Cockerell Bindery, Riversdale, Grantchester, Cambridge CB3 9NB

Dryad Press, Northgates, Leicester LE1 9BU

Russell Bookcrafts, Hitchin, Hertfordshire

Metric Conversion Chart

INCHES TO MILLIMETERS AND CENTIMETERS

(Measurements of less than an inch are rounded to the nearest half millimeter; measurements of an inch or more are rounded to the nearest half centimeter)

inches	mm	inches	cm	inches	cm	inches	cm
⅛	3	1	2.5	4	10	10	25.5
³⁄₁₆	4.5	1½	4	5	12.5	12	30.5
¼	6	2	5	6	15	15	38
⅜	9.5	2½	6.5	7	18	20	51
½	12.5	3	7.5	8	20.5	25	63.5
¾	17.5	3½	9	9	23	30	76

OUNCES TO GRAMS

(Slightly rounded off for convenience)

ounces	grams	ounces	grams
½	14	3	85
1	28	3½	100
1½	42	4	114
2	57	4½	128
2½	71	5	142

QUARTS TO LITERS

(Slightly rounded off for convenience)

quarts	liters	quarts	liters
1	.95	6	5.70
2	1.90	7	6.65
3	2.85	8	7.60
4	3.80	9	8.55
5	4.75	10	9.45

(You will probably find it easier to round the metric weight and volume equivalents to easily measurable amounts; for example: the 5 ounces of moss and 8 quarts of water used in the classic marbleizing size can be converted to 150 grams of moss and 8 liters of water.)